IS MY MICROPHONE ON?

ALSO BY JORDAN TANNAHILL

Age of Minority
Botticelli in the Fire & Sunday in Sodom
Concord Floral
Late Company

IS
MY
MICROPHONE
ON?

JORDAN TANNAHILL

PLAYWRIGHTS CANADA PRESS
TORONTO

Author photo © Caio Sanfelice

Playwrights Canada Press
202-269 Richmond St. W., Toronto, ON M5V 1X1
416.703.0013 | info@playwrightscanada.com | www.playwrightscanada.com

For professional or amateur production rights, please contact:
Colin Rivers at Marquis Entertainment
402-10 Adelaide St. East, Toronto, ON M5C 1J3
416-960-9123 X 223 | info@mqlit.ca

Library and Archives Canada Cataloguing in Publication
Title: Is my microphone on? / Jordan Tannahill.
Names: Tannahill, Jordan, author.
Description: A play.
Identifiers: Canadiana (print) 20220251827 | Canadiana (ebook) 20220251851
 | ISBN 9780369103734 (softcover) | ISBN 9780369103758 (PDF)
 | ISBN 9780369103741 (HTML)
Classification: LCC PS8639.A577 I8 2022 | DDC C812/.6—dc23

Playwrights Canada Press operates on land which is the ancestral home of the Anishinaabe Nations (Ojibwe / Chippewa, Odawa, Potawatomi, Algonquin, Saulteaux, Nipissing, and Mississauga), the Wendat, and the members of the Haudenosaunee Confederacy (Mohawk, Oneida, Onondaga, Cayuga, Seneca, and Tuscarora), as well as Metis and Inuit peoples. It always was and always will be Indigenous land.

We acknowledge the support of the Canada Council for the Arts, the Ontario Arts Council (OAC), Ontario Creates, and the Government of Canada for our publishing activities.

Is My Microphone On? was first produced in English by Canadian Stage, in High Park, Toronto, from September 2 to 19, 2021, with the following creative team:

Directed and Dramaturged by Erin Brubacher
Original Music by Veda Hille
Visual Design by Sherri Hay
Sound Design by Debashis Sinha
Lighting Design by Kaitlin Hickey
Choreography by Cara Spooner
Stage Management by Sandy Plunkett
Assistant Stage Management by Taryn Dougall
Youth Mentorship by Davinder Malhi and Sadie Laflamme-Snow

Performed by Remi Ajao-Russell, Hiyab Araya, Jack Bakshi, Chloe Cha, Felix Chew, Nia Downey, Sidonie Fleck, Oscar Gorbet, Saraphina Knights, Iris MacNada, Iylah Mohammed, Amaza Payne, Sanora Souphommanychanh, Alykhan Sunderji, Catherine Thorne, Sophia Wang, and Skyler Xiang

The play was simultaneously produced in German by Theater der Welt / Bürgerbühne und Junges Schauspiel des Düsseldorfer Schauspielhaus, Düsseldorf, Germany, by the following creative team:

Directed by Erin Brubacher and Bassam Ghazi
Original Music by Veda Hille
Music Direction by Hajo Wiesemann
Director's Assistants Solène Schlachter and Auguste Sandner
Translation by Frank Weigand
Dramaturgy by Erin Brubacher and Kirstin Hess

Performed by Nika Andabaka, Frida Beucker, Lucy Brouwers, Ayla Tatu Burnaz, Sofia Cuesta Fouß, Paula Darius, Phoenix Grün, Isoken Iyahen, Friederike Jacobs, Collins Kang, Fey Lawal, Hannah Juli Mellinghaus, Eleni Melikidou, Exalte Nsingi, Emir Özdemir, Maja Rabrenovic, Jakob Schiefer, and Tobi Valder

NOTES

This piece is intended for an ensemble of youth under the voting age in the country of its performance. The size of the ensemble is variable but should ideally be no fewer than seven.

The text was informed by the young people we worked with for the premiere productions in Düsseldorf and Toronto and was regularly edited to reflect current events and local perspectives. All future productions are encouraged to do the same.

The title *Is My Microphone On?* is inspired by a line from Greta Thunberg's speech to British MPs at the Houses of Parliament on April 23, 2019.

"Let me recite what history teaches" is from Gertrude Stein's poem "If I Told Him: A Completed Portrait of Picasso."

A backslash (/) within a line signals the start of the following line, thus creating an overlap.

An ensemble of young performers gradually enter a theatre.
There are several musical instruments on stage.

Lights shift.

They address the audience.

Check

One two

Check check one two

Can you hear me? Am I coming through?

Can we, sorry— Can we just test the drums?

   A performer tests the drums.

Is that amp on?

Can you turn it up?

   A performer turns up the amp.

   Two performers strum electric guitars.

And the bass?

Performer tests the bass guitar.

That's good

We want to make sure you can hear us

    A performer begins strumming the bass guitar.

(fellow performer's name) here is going to strum this guitar two hundred times tonight

Which is how many species will have gone extinct on Earth today

Within the last twenty-four hours

(fellow performer's name) has been playing the bass since she was eight

My dad taught me

By a show of hands, who in the audience is a Millennial?

    Wait for members of the audience to raise their hand.

Okay, a few of you, nice to see you

Thanks for coming

Who here is Gen X? Can you raise your hands?

    Wait for members of the audience to raise their hand.

Hi, Gen X

Thanks for Nirvana

And finally can all of the Baby Boomers raise your hands?

Wait for members of the audience to raise their hand.

Thank you for outing yourselves

Brave

We promise to go gentle on you tonight

Well

Not too gentle

To all the generations here tonight

All the adults

Hello

Welcome

We made this for you

Especially you

And for ourselves of course

But mostly to tell you

It's over

Your world

Your time is up

Mom

Dad

It's our turn

Dear Boomers

Gen X

Dear Mom and Dad

Millennials

Leave the keys on the counter

Gran

Your world is over

Your world

Leave the keys

This is no longer your world

Your time

Is up

Finished

From here on out

From this moment onwards

This is our world

Grandpa

We're in charge

This is an insurgency

This is a stick up

This is the end

This is where we begin

This is where we pick up

We're here to tell you

What we cannot tell you at the kitchen table

Or over the phone

Or in a text

To start

If nothing

If nothing else

You fucked up

Sorry to say

I know you tried

Some of you tried

But it wasn't enough

And frankly

I'm tired

Of your excuses

Your deflection

Throwing your hands up

I don't understand how you can still look me in the eye and say

"One day"

"You can be whatever you want to be"

"If you focus"

"One day"

"If you work hard"

"A teacher"

"A house"

I need you to understand when you talk about the future

And I'm serious about this

When you talk about the future

I have a hard time sometimes picturing myself getting there

And if not me, there are kids

Other kids

Maybe here in this room

Or other rooms, in this world

Who will not actually get there

Floods

Fire

Displacement

I'm not talking abstractly

I'm talking real things

Already happening

I'm talking about my actual future

The future

Of your children

Your friends' children

Neighbours

Children you don't know

Strangers

On the subway

In the park

In the parking lot of the mall

We may not

Actually

Get there

All because a handful of people

A few hundred men

Needed to make an impossible amount of money

And when I say "make"

No one "makes" a billion dollars

You steal a billion dollars

You steal lives

Futures

And our futures

Mom

Are being stolen

Right now

And in ten

Maybe fifteen years

We will reach a point of no return

An irreversible chain reaction

Each year the dry season gets dryer

Riverbeds

And scorched lawns

The baked earth

Where nothing goes to seed

Farm fields outside the city

Already dead by the start of summer

And then elsewhere

Towns

And cities

Whole coastlines

Under water

There was flooding around my grandparents' house this spring

Historic flooding

True story

They were trapped in their home, on the second floor, for a week with no electricity, no landline, no running water

They survived off cans of beans and tuna

A tin of apple juice

The fire department eventually boated in and rescued them

They were brought straight to the hospital and were put on IVs for dehydration

True story

Their house was totally ruined

It basically has to be gutted or torn down

All experts agree

All over the news they said

The flooding is climate-change related

And still

Still

My grandfather calls climate change "liberal mania"

Those were his actual words

Mania?

Grandpa, you literally don't have a house

Three storms of the century in the last three years, back-to-back

Like—?

How can we talk?

What language?

What words?

If you don't want to listen

Do I have to speak louder?

Grandma?

Do I have to light flares?

Do I have to glue myself to the road?

Do I have to glue my hands to the sidewalk?

Do I have to glue myself to the doors?

Do I have to set myself on fire?

Do I have to glue myself to the airplane?

Do I have to glue / myself to the runway?

Do I have to glue myself to the doors of the stock exchange?

Do I have to glue myself to the doors / of Shell Oil?

Do I have to glue myself / to the boardroom table?

Do I have to glue myself to / the top of a subway car?

Do I have to set myself on fire?

Do I have to glue myself to / the doors of the bank?

Do I have to glue myself to your SUV?

Do I have to glue myself / to the pipeline?

Do I have to / glue myself to your yacht?

Do I have to set myself on fire?

Grandma

Grandma, let me be clear

I want you to live

When the pandemic came, we sacrificed

We stopped the world for you

I stopped my life

Because I wanted you to live

What about us?

Do you want the same for me?

This is about lives

This is about our lives

Mom

Dad

If I said to you, tonight: you're failing us

Do you hear me?

Do you accept that?

You are failing

You have failed us

You are failures

And this madness

This blindness

This not-seeing

Not-doing

This business-as-usual

Will be remembered in history as one of the greatest failures of humankind

18

You will be remembered

As one of the greatest failures of mankind

I told my mom yesterday over breakfast

"You're a failure"

She didn't like that

She said: "Well what's your solution?"

I said: "I'm twelve"

I said

"We could stop burning fossil fuels"

That's a start

She said: "Yeah, we've already thought of that"

"Believe it or not"

My dad said

"Maybe instead of striking, you could stay in school and come up with a solution"

I said, "Go fuck yourself"

I'm joking

I definitely didn't say that

That would not have gone over well

Well we could end capitalism

My mom rolled her eyes

"Please"

"You can't just say that"

My dad said

"You can't just say"

"End capitalism"

Why not?

"Because you benefit from it"

"It gives you the life you have"

"That cereal you're eating"

"That toast"

"That orange juice"

Yeah, but what if we could have another life?

What if there was another way to be?

"You can't just say 'end capitalism'" my dad said

"Besides"

My mom said

"You just can't"

"It's not possible"

"That's like saying: end oxygen"

End sadness

End the night

There are some things that are beyond us

Like God

Like cities

They operate completely of their own volition

You can't stop people from dying

Or eating

Or crying

"You can't stop capitalism," she said

"Not by yourself, at least"

My dad laughed

Well I'm not by myself

I said

Look

I'm not by myself

Look

Look at us

Here we are

Who said I was by myself?

Look

In the street

Look at us trying

We could

Maybe

Find another way

I start talking about circular economy

And rewilding nature

Forests

Mangroves

Seagrass meadows

Humans are very adaptable, Mom

And we still have some time

But not long

You want solutions that let you live like before

Live like now

But those don't exist anymore

Because we didn't act in time

You say: "Well we compost, we recycle"

"We bring our own bags to the store"

You taught us this was about individual responsibility

But then I look up and watch a billionaire burn a hundred thousand gallons of rocket fuel for a ten-minute joyride

I open Twitter and I see the Gulf of Mexico on fire

The ocean literally on fire

It's got to be a lot more than just composting, Mom

My brother was there at breakfast

He said, "God you're annoying"

"So self-righteous"

My sister

She's a bit older than me

She gets it

Mine does too

She's a bit younger

We're the same age

My brother—

He gets it

As kids we fought each other

I fought her all the time

Pulled her hair

She pushed me into a wall

The fridge

Slammed my head into the fridge

She threw dirt in my eyes

I broke her nose

Really?

With a stone

Your sister?

Yeah well she poured water on my laptop

Shit

I have three brothers and we—

We were always at each other's throats

This scar here?

This is from my brother

He bit me

I broke a plate on his head

We fought for everything

The front seat

The remote

The swing

The last slice of pizza

Of cake

Now we're fighting you

Now we're fighting for our lives

I have this memory of coming downstairs one night

And you and Mom were watching a movie on the couch

A disaster movie

And you said go back to bed

It's too scary

Cities under water

Cities on fire

Cities getting blown away

It's not for kids

You said the movie would keep us awake

But now

It's not a movie

There's no special effects

But you were right about one thing

Mom

Dad

We're awake

We are very much awake

Ever since I was little I've had dreams about a tornado

Wake up

It's always the same dream

There are dark clouds on the horizon

Lightning is hitting the ground all around me

And the finger of God pokes down through the clouds and starts sucking up all the land it touches. It starts coming toward me, and I start running. I'm running through the park. Down the street. Toward my house. The tornado is coming for me, I can hear its scream. And as I get near my house, I can see my parents standing in the doorway shouting. They're shouting at me, "Hurry, run, run faster." But as I reach the door, they close it. In my face. I try to open it, but it's locked. They've locked it, and they're already hiding in the basement

Wake up

> *Another performer begins strumming an electric guitar. She will continue to do so every fifteen seconds throughout the show.*

Every time *(fellow performer's name)* strums this guitar

Every fifteen seconds

Another three thousand trees are cut down

Clear-cut

Cedar

Pine

Palm

Acacia

My mom tells me I shouldn't worry

"What good will worrying do?"

But you know what, Mom?

Dad?

I want you to worry

Worry about the future

About the tipping point

Because

Dad

I'm panicking

Sometimes

Some mornings

A full-on attack

On the bus

In the shower

I have to sit down

And let the water fall over me

"Get ahold of yourself"

My mom says

"Get some perspective"

"Just breathe"

"Just calm down"

But, Mom

It's time to panic

"I have enough to panic about, thank you"

"Taxes"

"The car"

"Traffic"

I know but—

"Dinner plans"

"We're late"

"Grandpa's in the hospital"

Okay but—

"Let's go, get in the car"

What about the ice caps?

What?

The bees

The shoreline

My dad says

"What am I supposed to do about the goddamn bees?"

Dad, I'm literally losing sleep

"Well don't"

Don't what?

"Don't lose sleep over the goddamn bees"

Dad, the fire is coming, can't you see?

The line of smoke

Can't you see?

The birds

Taking flight

Run

My whole life I've been

Running

Fast as I can

Running

My whole life

Not long

I haven't lived

Very long

My whole life

I've been running

To seek

To hide

Running away from

The fire

Running toward the light

Running from you

Running to

Catch the bus

Catch a break

Running

Until my lungs burned

Running across

The face of the Earth

To breathlessness

To burning

The lungs

Of the Earth

Breathless

Burning

The Amazon

Banyan trees

Rubber trees

A football field a second

Can you run that fast?

A football field a second?

You tell me I oversimplify

You tell me

I can't do anything about it

I'm just a child

Sixteen

Fourteen

You tell me to go back to school

You tell me

I'm not saying anything new

But what are you doing?

Why aren't you doing anything?

Do something

Anything

For fuck sake

And until you do

We will

Until you do

We will flip our desks

We will

Throw our papers

And pull the alarm

Until you do

Pull the alarm

The schools will be empty

Until something changes

Pull the alarm

And if all our leaders can do is offer us words

And good intentions

Vote them out

The business as usual

Vote it out

When you have trash

Throw it out

And if you don't

We will

It wasn't us who voted them in

It wasn't our vote

And we're calling bullshit

The people in power

The people you voted in

One day

We're going to throw them out

Politicians saying we don't know what we're talking about

We're too young to know how government works

Throw them out

Mom

Dad

You say to me

I'm only going to say this once

I'm not going to repeat myself

Well

I'm only going to say this once

So I hope you're listening

This is a declaration of war

And you started it

No

You lit the fires

Not war

Yes

Yes, war

You didn't think this moment would come?

You can't say they lit the fires

No more than you have

Don't call it a war

Listen

Mom

You know what I'm talking about

Stop the banks

Put away your guns

Stop Facebook

My intention is to live

My intention is to live a good life on Earth

My intention is to grow old and die

I kinda like Facebook

Me too

Facebook is dead

Facebook is our fault

No, Facebook is Millennial

Fuck Facebook

Yeah, Mark Zuckerberg is not our fault

None of this is our fault

Of course it is

It's not

Oh come on

You think TikTok is better?

You think our kids won't be talking to us like this?

Or their kids?

What sacrifices are you going to make?

Yeah

I make sacrifices

What, you put your computer on dark mode?

He only uses one square of toilet paper to wipe his ass

Shut up

You just told me you went to Croatia

Yeah, because we have family there

So?

We go every year

Exactly, what the hell is that?

We're visiting family. / It's not like it's vacation.

So? It doesn't matter

It's family

We don't even have a choice, our parents make us

People should be limited to one flight a year

What?

One long-haul flight a year

You can't say that

People don't need more than that

You can't limit / people's freedom of mobility

You want a police state?

It's a basic human right

It's a privilege, not a right

Uh—

Freedom of movement is a right

Not the freedom to fly all over the world as much as you want whenever you want

You have no idea what you're talking about

You sound just like my dad

My dad says, "What do you know?"

"What do you know?"

"What have you seen?"

"To talk to me"

"Me"

"An adult"

"This way"

And I say

Well

I once saw a boy drop a heavy rock off an overpass—

I once saw a man punch a woman—

—and it hit the windshield of a car passing below

—She was my mother

I once drowned in the water park

But they brought me back to life

Bodies have been inside my body

And I have been outside

Of my body

I've seen my blood

On a man's hands

I've seen blood

On every surface

I've seen my parents watching television in the living room

And imagined them as corpses

Lying side by side in their coffins

White light flickering

On their faces

Like death

I've seen a turtle run over by a car

I have seen the darkness

My sister

I've wiped the tears

From her cold cheek

The grease

Off her dirty face

You think I don't know?

Dad

The wind is moving at three metres a second today

And you think

What is the wind exactly?

And how have I gotten so old without knowing?

I wish you would teach me about that

I wish you would teach me how to live without shame

I wish you would teach me fragility

I wish you would teach me about your first heartbreak

One day

I will not think you know everything

Or even as much as me

Or maybe much at all

I will be disappointed

In you

In myself

For trusting you

I will have to change my thinking

Realize I am the adult

I am the one taking care of you

I don't hate you because you're weak

Or because you're scared

Or because you're wrong

I told my dad: "I know you're older than me in this life, I grant you that"

But who knows how long it's taken our souls to get here?

There was one life I lived where I was a dog. I was owned by a family and they were very good to me

And there was another life when I was a car. And this man drove around inside of me, just going to different appointments and stuff. And then he got rid of me, and I was in a junkyard for years. Just years and years sitting there, underneath all of these other crushed cars, because even though they crushed me into a cube, my soul was still stuck inside

And then in another life I was like a . . . a small bubble of foam on a wave coming to shore, and the wave broke, and I burst, and that was it, it was very quick

But before that I was a small stream, for centuries

And in another life I was a mortal girl

Which is this life

And in this life, I finally have the power to speak

After thousands of years

I have a mouth

I have words

So if you don't mind

Mom

Dad

I'm going to speak

I'm going to shout

When I become a human

I'm going use some words

Can you still hear me?

Is my microphone on?

Check

Check one two

Shout out to my mom

Shout out to the moms here tonight

Shout out to my followers

Shout out to the snowflakes

Shout out to the strikers

Shout out to those who walked out

Text me when you're home safe

I posted this photo of me with this guy I'm seeing

And my mom commented below: "You need a job, Lauren, not a boyfriend"

Brutal

My mom sent me a text

"Why're you tweeting like you're famous? You have maybe seven active followers"

Blocked

Shout out to the dead

How do you tell your mom you've got a hammer stuck in your mouth?

Shout out to the angels

Do you ever just realize that your mom is a living, breathing angel and feel really bad for being so shit to her when you were fifteen?

I asked my mom what I should be for Halloween

And she said:

"I don't know, what's popular among your generation?"

Apparently Xanax wasn't the right answer

Tyler started a live video

Watch it before it ends

Marika started a live video

Thomas started a live video

Watch it before the world ends

Shout out to the people arrested on the bridge

Ahmed started a live video

Shout out to Greta

Shout out to AOC

She said shake the table

To the girls who spoke up

Shake the table

Sometimes ladies

It's not enough just to get a seat at the table

Sometimes

You need to shake the table

Shake

Shake the table

Here's to real justice

Justice for the water we drink

Real justice

Justice for our air we breathe

Shake

Justice for how much women get paid

Yes

And for the workers without protections

Justice for the non-human beings

I want justice for the oceans

And the forests

And the farmers

Sometimes

You need to shake the table

I'm only going to say this once

You say

You say I have nothing to complain about

Shake

That we have more things than you ever had

More education

No smallpox

We'll live past a hundred

No Mao Zedong

Better nutrition

What do we have to complain about?

If you're a woman

If you're queer

Why are you complaining?

Shake the table

It's a privilege

You say

To skip school

To protest

Privilege?

We're spoiled

Ungrateful

You say

We're entitled

You want to tell me clean drinking water

Clean air

Is that a privilege now?

Excuse me?

Whose privilege is the Amazon?

Whose privilege is the coral reef?

Whose cities are disposable?

Whose bodies?

Whose countries?

Who lives in the sacrifice zone?

Who lives beside the toxic e-dumps?

The piles of burning computers?

Who mines the coltan for our phones?

The lead

The mercury

Shake

Who's collateral?

Shake

Who's on the front lines?

Who's always on the front lines?

Shake the table

Shake shake shake

Yourself

Shake awake, Mom

Shake the trunk

Shake the roots

Shake awake

Shake the night

Shake the city

Shake its doubt

If you were waiting for a time

The time is now

If you were waiting for a line

The line has been drawn

If you were waiting for others, they are waiting for you

> *A performer begins strumming another electric guitar every five seconds.*

Every time *(performer's name)* strums this guitar

Once every five seconds

A million tons of ice collapses

From the ice caps

And melts into the ocean

I've never seen it

The ocean

Really?

I've never seen the ocean

Not yet

My parents took me camping there once

There were cliffs

Quite high

I mean—relatively

My father asked

"Have you ever seen the sun rise over the water?"

I said, "I don't think so"

He said, "You have to wake up early"

Okay then

Wake me up, in the morning

I want to be there when the sun rises

And so he set his alarm

And we woke up—

—so tired—

—just before dawn

The birds

Everything was cold

The wind

He wrapped me in a blanket

Over my shoulders

We walked to the edge of the cliff and looked out

And we watched the sun rise together over the water

It was—

It really was incredible

And I felt very close to him

In that moment

I felt very much

In the world

In love with

Being in the world

Like a very small thing

With not much time

Poor Dad

Am I your child?

Am I the thing you wanted?

Am I your wish fulfilled?

All the questions I've ever asked you

Is it getting dark?

Is my head bleeding?

Is it time yet?

Is it time to go?

Is time linear?

Is it worth it?

Is life—?

Is all this pain?

And will it get better?

And if not now, when?

And if not for your love

And if not for the night

If not for the cities

And the streets

When they empty

And all the things you've said to me, Mom

As I walk out the door

"Hold on"

"Lemme give you a kiss"

"You have something on your face"

"Your hair"

(in annoyed tone) Mom

Lick your hand

And slick it down

"There you go"

She just wants the best for me

She says

"I just want the best for you"

She says

Well, Mom

I just want to live

I want to live to see a seagrass meadow

I want to live to see my daughter

I want my daughter to live to see

A seagrass meadow

I want my daughter's daughter to live to see

A forest

A mangrove

I want to live

I want to live to see my daughter's daughter

I want to live

It's hard to live in a broken world

When you're broken

I want to live

Last year I was in a really dark relationship

Like really dark

He was older than me

How much?

Like illegal older?

I guess so, yeah

He was an addict

He used to hit me, and steal things from me

And my mom kept telling me: "Just stop"

Just stop seeing him

But I couldn't because I was scared

But also it was how I knew how to feel good

We had good sex

He made me feel loved

And I guess I was addicted to him

What I'm saying is—

—sometimes I think it's hard to stop doing the thing that's destroying you. You know? Like humans? I get it

Forgive yourselves

You're broken

I know because I was broken

You're broken

Forgive yourselves

But also get your shit together. Give up your addictions

Oil

They're going to kill you

Beef

You know that they are

Sometimes it's hard to stop doing the thing that's destroying you

When it's the only way you know how to feel good

Or safe

Secure

The crazy things you do to feel secure

Like voting for fascists

Mom

What is it with your generation and fascists?

Look at the numbers

We're not the ones voting for them

Dad

Please

Stop

Stop voting for fascists

Look at the numbers

It's not us

It's you

Read our lips

Stop

Voting

For fascists

Britain

America

Why is that your solution?

Brazil

Do they make you feel more secure?

Poland

Hungary

France

Is it because of refugees?

Globalization?

Are you feeling unsteady in your old age?

Impotent?

You need someone to hold your dick?

Let me recite what history teaches

Watch for the signs

Mom

Because I don't think you're watching

And maybe, Dad

You've forgotten what they are

Please watch for the signs

Watch for the changing of the guard

Watch for the power grab

Watch when they name the enemy

And try to rally you around it

Watch for the rallies

Watch the military

Watch what they do

Watch the elections

Watch the journalists

And the intellectuals

And what happens to them

Watch what the scientists can say

And not say

Watch the rich

Watch for the money changing hands

Watch what happens at night

When nobody is watching

Watch the conspiracies

Watch the churches

Watch the prisons

Watch the schools

Watch what is said

And done

To women

Watch for the signs, Mom

Because I don't think you are

The way you talk about other immigrants

Dad

Makes me think you don't know

Makes me think you can't see

What is happening

Makes me angry

Makes me think you've forgotten

What history teaches

Remember

What happens over there in the desert

Happens in your backyard

What happens on the screen

Happens in real life

What happens to your neighbour

Happens to you

This is the sign

The sign is death

Can I ask you, Dad

What is a country?

I know you love our country

Flags

Borders

Anthems

But what is a country?

I have a feeling

When the world floods there will be no countries

When the world floods

There will be no borders

And when the world burns

There will be no borders

No wall can keep the fire out

No wall can keep the people out

I have a feeling

The Earth does not know the name of our country

The Earth does not know

Its shape on the map

And in several thousand years, no one will

Almost like it was never there

Almost like it was something we made up

You say you're a reasonable person, Dad

Reasonable people

Doing reasonable things

Good people

Salt of the earth

Just trying to get by

Tell me: What's reasonable?

Dad

Walls?

Camps?

These seem reasonable

To reasonable people

Good ideas

To good people

One morning you're standing at the window watching our neighbour in her garden and you say

"I'd like you to go next door and help her for a bit"

What?

Why?

"Because she's old"

"She's a good person"

Why is she a good person?

Because she smiles at you?

Because she has a garden?

Dad, she's a racist

"No she's not"

She told me never trust Muslims

"Yes, but"

She's homophobic

"I'm sure she doesn't have any problem with you"

She doesn't have a clue!

She's always asking if I have a boyfriend

"She's always been very sweet"

Yeah, you're white, middle class, straight

"All right, enough"

I'm just saying—

"She's almost eighty"

So?

Does that make her a good person?

Because she's old?

Because she bakes for you at Christmas?

Fuck her

"Excuse me?"

She's a pig

Let her crawl around in the dirt

You said that?

To your dad?

Nazis had gardens too

Whoa

Yup

I could not say that to my dad

Hell no

Do you not get it? Maybe I've been mincing my words. I hate you. I hate old people. I literally hate you. You have fucked up this world. For us. Forever. At least for a very, very long time. And, what, we're just supposed to forgive you? Because you're cute? Fragile? Toothless? Senile? Because you knit? And do crosswords? And go on package holidays and take photographs with your stupid cameras in your big shorts? I am literally filled with rage when I see you. I want to shove your faces in the dirt of your gardens. I'm not going to stand up for you on the fucking bus. I'm not going to hold the door open for you, or talk to you about the weather, or smile as you count your change forever at the counter, all the change you have in your pockets, all the money in the fucking world that you earned when you walked out of college, with half my education, into a high-paid job with full benefits, and then voted in governments, one after the other, that stripped away workers' benefits and job security. And now I'll have to work two, three, four jobs earning a fraction of what you did, and you call us lazy, narcissistic. I'm not going listen to you complain about the price of tomatoes and lettuce in the grocery stores when—you know who's keeping those prices low? All the migrants who fled war zones who you don't want in the country, who are bent over in the dirt not, no, not weeding their flower gardens, but trying to make enough money to keep their families alive. You tell me you don't recognize your country anymore. All these new faces. New languages. New gadgets. They scare you. So you vote in people who tell you they're going to wind back the clock. Take us back to the glory days when people like you were carefree and oblivious, and we were beaten up in the fucking streets for being Black, or Asian, for being a faggot, and kept out of jobs for being a woman, and raped without recourse. So no. I'm sorry. I'm not going to help you pluck weeds out of your fucking garden

    Silence.

I think that's really shit

Me too

Like—

Personally, I think we should respect our elders

Why?

What've they done to deserve it?

I love my grandparents

Live a long time?

I love my grandparents too but—

Hoard money?

—I don't have to respect their messed-up views

My neighbour—

They have knowledge to impart

So do we

Sure, but—

So do people they think shouldn't be in our country

But talk to them

Don't shut them out

Yeah I do

I do talk to them

And I'm horrified by what comes out of their decrepit mouths

My neighbour, she was old, like about seventy-seven or something.
And like she actually died in the pandemic

What? Seriously?

Yeah, like actually died of it. Because she used to volunteer a lot, like at
my school. And when my mom was getting chemotherapy, this woman
used to drive her to appointments at the hospital because my dad was
working

Listen, I'm not saying old people aren't nice—

I was so sad

My grandmother's an activist

So don't generalize

I'm just expressing what I feel, okay?

Well

So fuck off. I'm sorry, but I don't think it's without truth

It's not productive

At all

The opposite, actually

Like—dangerous

Well

It is

We need a way forward

The rich are oppressors, not the elderly

Yes

You think it's easy being old? The elderly get treated like shit

Yeah the thing is

The truth is

We probably need to kill the one percent

No—

If we're going to survive

—that's not what I'm saying

We need

Violent insurrection

Come on

That's not funny

I don't condone violence

Violence is sometimes / a necessary means to an end

Unavoidable

Violence

Real change

Violence is never the answer

If we're going to survive

Even just the upper .5%

They need to be killed

That probably means some of you

They'll just be replaced

Guys, seriously

No purges

That's not something to joke about

I wasn't joking

Why should there be billionaires?

It's obscene

No violence

Their wealth is a violence

That wealth—?

That is violence

That kind of wealth—?

A billion dollars? Is criminal

Honestly, if I could—

If I could I'd burn down their mansions

Me too

Firebomb them

Molotov

Set Amazon on fire

Ha

Burn Amazon

Or

Or turn their mansions into something like, you know—

Homeless shelters

Or like free daycares

Honestly, billionaires—?

Drag them out

They should be fucking dragged out of their spaceships

But

And strung up

Jeff Bezos

Tied to a lamppost

Guys

With shit stuffed in his mouth

His own shit

No, your shit

I'd shove my shit in Jeff Bezos's mouth

Just shut up

You shut up

We need a way forward

We need revolution

You say you don't want violence?

I'm saying—

You don't get to say that. You don't get to say "I don't want violence."
Tell the people of Dhaka that, when their city is under water. When the
slums of Lagos and Jakarta are under water, tell them "no violence."
This is a violence. We are a violence. Us sitting here in Toronto, this
theatre, our privilege, our clothes, our power, this is a violence, we are
a violence. And trust me, when the crops fail, and the fields are burning, and the water is rising, there will be violence. And it will stay over
there for a while. But one day, it will come here. It will come here, with
bodies, and faces, and names. Because the violence has always existed,
and it has always been ours. We have just pretended not to notice

But I still think—

You don't think the rich know that there'll be violence? You don't think
the billionaires have been preparing? Amazon, Google—

Building armies

Huawei

Collecting our data

Armies?

They'll be more powerful than governments

Mr. Conspiracy

They already are

Education, health care, building roads—

Armies, though?

Drones

No

I'd still say hope—

Facial recognition

—hope is stronger than violence

Tell that to the dying

Hope is stronger than fear

Hope is your privilege

This is a revolution of compassion

This

This is a revolution—

Yes

—of tenderness

Human-scaled

Human to human-scaled

When I become human—

Not of despair or rage or / whatever fear you're peddling

There's already rage

And what conquers rage?

Rage is rage

What conquers rage?

Oh please, don't—don't give me that "hope" bullshit. Your hope is inaction. Your hope is lazy and weak. Your hope is the hope that someone else will sort it out and / that you can go on living your same life

My hope is that our compassion for one another, for the earth

For your children

Supersedes your fear and mistrust

Supersedes your greed

Supersedes

Viciousness

And cowardice

And guilt

Supersedes

Our shame

Our always wanting

Wanting and

Craving

Yearning

Our never understanding ourselves

And hurling ourselves into death

When I become a human, I want to remember what it was not to be human. I want to remember the time I spent as a rock. As a stream. As a piece of trash on the highway. I want to remember what it was to have no say. When I become a human, I want to be a healer. A doctor, maybe. Or someone who holds other people when they cry. When I become a human, I want to be patient and gentle. I want to remember names. Colours of people's eyes. Colours of the sky, at different times of day. The smell of certain trees. Certain times of year. When I finally get the chance to become human, I'm going to spend some time using my voice. To sing. To talk. To make myself understood. Before people had microphones, they just held their hands up to their mouths like this and spoke very loudly. And maybe, before microphones, people just had to listen to each other just a little bit harder. A little bit more carefully. Animals, if they don't listen, they die. Death will creep up behind them when they're least expecting. When I become human, I'm going to listen. Every day that I'm human— Every single day—

Every day

A performer begins playing a kick drum every two seconds. It creates a rhythmic undertone.

Every time *(fellow performer's name)* hits that drum

We need—

Another four million pounds of CO_2 is released into the atmosphere

   A performer begins playing something on a synth.

Every time *(fellow performer's name)* plays the synth

We need a way forward

   A performer begins to sing a melody.

Every time *(fellow performer's name)* sings

Every time there is music

Every time we don't give up

Every time

Every day

Every moment of every day

Every moment there is hope

Every shred of hope left

Every one of us

Every second of the day

If you're still able

To wake up in the morning

If the morning

If there is still the morning

If you can get out of bed

If light

If there is still light

If the birds come

And don't hit the glass

If the birds and the ice come

And don't melt in your glass

If the day lasts

And the sun sets

If the day closes into night

If there is laughter

If there is

If you are still there

Dad

If at the end of the day

If you're still there

If your arms

If time

In your loving arms

If in time

If there is a way forward

There must be

A way forward

And if the rain

And if the city

And even in the flood

If you still love me

If I'm your child

 The music stops.

 A silence.

 Eventually . . .

Check

Check one

Check one two

Can you hear me?

Are you still listening?

    Pause.

I think we're all trying our best

Not hard enough

Will we be any better?

When we're sitting where they are now, and our children are here talking to us?

What will we have done?

It's hard

The way forward—

I know you're trying

Like really hard

When you feel—

The only way forward—

—insignificant

—is urgent togetherness

Urgent—?

Togetherness. We are all in this together—urgently, passionately, presently

Here

Now

Hurting

Yes

Hurting very much

Okay

Angry

Perhaps, but—

Working through

Working through it

Toward

Some progress

Is possible

Maybe even tonight

When I look in your eyes

Maybe even some

Small

Breakthrough

Tonight

When I look in your eyes

Mom

Dad

I know

I know you're doing your best

It's not good enough

I know

It has to get better

But I love you

> *Pause.*

I love you

> *Pause.*

I love you too

Gran

I love you

My neighbours

Teachers

I love you

Truck drivers

Doctors

The workers at the docks

I love you

My hairdresser and—

Farmers

—the garbage collectors

Adults I've never met

The old woman on the bus

The nurses in the hospital

Executives—

The men in the forests—

—in their suits

—with chainsaws

Even them

I love you

And I forgive you

I forgive you

I forgive you

I forgive all of you

I forgive you

I forgive you but

I don't accept

We forgive you

But we don't accept

You are human

Move past this anger

I'm still angry

Move past it

What you have done is forgiven—

We forgive you

—but it is not acceptable

We do not accept it

You must know

You are forgiven

But what you have done is unacceptable

There can be forgiveness

Without acceptance

It's the only way forward

Tonight

I look you in the eye

And you see me for the first time

Tonight

I look you in the eye

We're on the same side

Tonight I look you in the eye

You die, I die

Tonight

I look you in the eye

What will it take?

Tonight I look you in the eye

What took you so long?

Tonight

I look you in the eye

We're on the same side

Tonight

I look you in the eye

You die, I die

Tonight

We forgive you

But we don't accept

Tonight

Set your alarm

I want to be there when the sun rises

Mom

Dad

Set your alarm

I want to be there

When the sun rises

In the dead of the night

Wake up

It's time to get up

Before the dark

Before the birds

And move with me

By your side

It's time

To be in the world

To be

In love with being in the world

To be a very small thing

With not much time

Wake up

I said

I want to be there when the sun rises

Wake up

This is the alarm

I want to be there

When the sun rises

Wake up

I want to be there tomorrow

I want to be there

The day after

And the day after that

This is the alarm

I want to be there when the sun rises

I want to be there

I want to be there

I want to be there

   Blackout.

HEARTFELT GRATITUDE TO . . .

Erin Brubacher, Veda Hille, Sherri Hay, Debashis Sinha, Kaitlin Hickey, Cara Spooner, Stefan Schmidtke, Kirstin Hess, Frank Weigand, Bassam Ghazi, Brendan Healy, Sandy Plunkett, Taryn Dougall, Davinder Malhi, Sadie Laflamme-Snow, Hajo Wiesemann, Solène Schlachter, Auguste Sandner, Remi Ajao-Russell, Hiyab Araya, Jack Bakshi, Chloe Cha, Felix Chew, Nia Downey, Sidonie Fleck, Oscar Gorbet, Saraphina Knights, Iris MacNada, Iylah Mohammed, Amaza Payne, Sanora Souphommanychanh, Alykhan Sunderji, Catherine Thorne, Sophia Wang, Skyler Xiang, Nika Andabaka, Frida Beucker, Lucy Brouwers, Ayla Tatu Burnaz, Sofia Cuesta FouB, Paula Darius, Pheonix Grün, Isoken Iyahen, Friederike Jacobs, Collins Kang, Fey Lawal, Hannah Juli Mellinghaus, Eleni Melikidou, Exalte Nsingi, Emir Özdemir, Maja Rabrenovic, Jakob Schiefer, Tobi Valder, Annie Gibson, Blake Sproule, Jessica Lewis, Imogen Sarre, Colin Rivers, Eric Kostiuk Williams, Canadian Stage, Theater der Welt, Bürgerbühne und Junges Schauspiel des Düsseldorfer Schauspielhauses, the National Theatre's Connections Festival, Edward Bromberg, Greta Thunberg, the Fridays For Future climate strikers, Extinction Rebellion, and to every land and environmental defender living, deceased, and yet to be born.

Jordan Tannahill is a playwright, author, and director of film and theatre. Jordan's plays have been translated into nine languages and twice honoured with a Governor General's Literary Award for Drama: in 2014 for *Age of Minority: Three Solo Plays* and in 2018 for *Botticelli in the Fire & Sunday in Sodom*. His first novel, *Liminal*, won France's Prix des jeunes libraires, and his second novel, *The Listeners*, was a finalist for the 2021 Giller Prize. In 2019, CBC Arts named Tannahill as one of sixty-nine LGBTQ Canadians, living or deceased, who has shaped the country's history.